MW00748544

Remembrance Day

Grades K-3

Written by Ruth Solski
Illustrated by S&S Learning Materials

ISBN 1-55035-742-5
Remembrance Day, SSC1-44
Copyright 2003 S&S Learning Materials
15 Dairy Avenue
Napanee, Ontario
K7R 1M4
All Rights Reserved * Printed in Canada
A Division of the Solski Group

Published in Canada by:
S&S Learning Materials
15 Dairy Avenue
Napanee, Ontario
K7R 1M4
www.sslearning.com

Look for Other Seasonal Resources

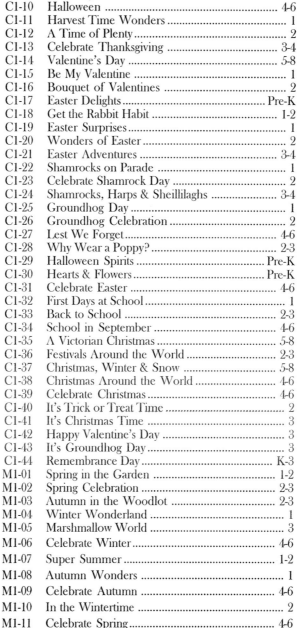

Published by:
S&S Learning Materials
15 Dairy Avenue
Napanee, Ontario
K74 1M4

© S&S Learning Materials

2

SSC1-44

Remembrance Day

Table of Contents

Remembrance Day

Learning Expectations

The information and activities about Remembrance Day are designed to help students achieve the following:

- to recognize the sacrifice made by thousands of Canadians in the First and Second World Wars and the Korean War.
- to develop an understanding of the significance of Remembrance Day.
- to develop an awareness of the ceremonies and rites of the past as they are reflected in the present.
- to appreciate the realities and complexities of war.
- to appreciate the qualities of endurance and courage, and of devotion to the principles of freedom within our multicultural society.
- to learn to resolve conflict successfully.
- to celebrate and appreciate peace.

List of Vocabulary

Remembrance Day Words:

November, World War I, World War II, Korean War, troops, soldiers, infantry, men, pilots, sailors, monument, cenotaph, poppy, Royal Canadian Legion, Peace Tower, The National War Memorial, Flanders Field, crosses, wreath, veterans, march, parades, bands, choirs, Two-Minute Silence, bugle, bugler, Last Post, Reveille, D-Day, army, airforce, marines, navy, Red Cross, memory, remember, praise, dead, laud, honour, fought, war, deed, cemetery, hero, heroism, heroic, pride, devotion, virile, gallant, valiant, aloof, sacrifice, tyranny, oppression, freedom, dignity, homage, courage, devotion, duty, tribute, dedicate, brave, bravery, victory, victors, allies, defeat, proud, surrender, loyalty, valour, respect

Famous Countries and Cities:

Normandy, Pearl Harbor, Nagasaki, Dunkirk, England, London, France, Paris, Belgium, Holland, Germany, Berlin, Hiroshima, Tokyo, Japan, Moscow, Russia, Poland, Warsaw

Famous War Leaders:

Adolph Hitler, Winston Churchill, Benito Mussolini, Franklin D. Roosevelt, Hideki Tojo

Military Equipment:

tanks, airplanes, jeeps, warships, aircraft, aircraft carriers, artillery, guns, bayonet, helmet, uniform, atomic bomb, bombs, grenade, buzz bombs, arms, shells, gas masks, radar, submarines, machine gun, torpedoes

Remembrance Day

Other War Words:

air raid siren, prisoner of war, prison camps, concentration camps, trenches, "Kamikazi", "blitzkrieg", "blitz", battle, front, fight, kill, wound, destroy, shoot, bomb, spy, defend, attack, battlefield, wounded, captured

Teacher Input Suggestions

Length of Time:

This theme may be used during the entire month of November. It does not have to dwell on the ugly aspects of war but on peace, friendship, respect, honour, the brotherhood of man, heroism, solving problems, getting along, etc.

Planning Ahead:

Look for the following items prior to the theme.

Pictures and Photographs of the Peace Tower, the National Memorial Monument, the real Poppy, war scenes, military personnel, cenotaphs, monuments, memorials, military equipment, Flanders Fields, war heroes, buildings destroyed by war, Remembrance Day ceremonies, military parades, veterans, war leaders

Films, filmstrips, and videos that pertain to World War I, World War II and the Korean War.

Books that show the three wars, military equipment, countries where the wars were fought, war leaders, war heroes. Locate books that relate heroic deeds to read to your class.

Discussion Topics:

The selection of topics and the depth in which they are discussed is left to the discretion of the teacher.

- What is a War? - causes
- World War I - causes, countries involved, results of the war, Canada's involvement
- World War II - causes, countries involved, results of the war, Canada's involvement
- Korean War - causes, countries involved, results of the war, Canada's involvement
- Famous War Leaders from World War I and World War II - Winston Churchill, Adolph Hitler, Benito Mussolini, Hideki Tojo, Franklin D. Roosevelt
- Peace - Peace Keeping Organizations, The United Nations, The Noble Peace Prize, Lester B. Pearson, Canadian Peace Keeping Operations, The International Law of Peace
- Freedom and Its Importance, Countries that do not have the same freedoms as Canada, example: Cuba, China, Korea, Russia
- Symbols of Peace - dove, white flag, olive branch, the Tree of the Great Peace 1390, Calumet or Peace Pipe, peace offering, Peace International Bridge, The International Peace Gardens
- Respect - how to show respect, why it is important

Remembrance Day

- Heroism and Heroic Deeds - brainstorm heroic acts, the attributes of a hero
- Memories - brainstorm for important memories, discuss war memories and their effects on people

Literature Ideas:

1. Choose a novel that pertains to families that lived during a wartime era to read to your class during the month of December.

   Some examples are:

   - Sadako and the 1000 Paper Cranes by Eleanor Coerr
   - Number the Stars by Lois Lowry
   - Rilla of Ingleside by Lucy Maud Montgomery
   - Snow Treasure by Marie McSwigan

2. Read poetry about heroic deeds, Remembrance Day, battles, war, life during the war etc. The following poems you might find useful.

The Cross

At the top of the hill
Stood a cross of white.
It gave me a chill
When I looked at this sight.

On the cross was a name
Of a soldier who had died.
Not knowing from where he came
Made me feel so sad inside.

Ruth Solski

The Airplane

The airplane taxis down the field
And heads into the breeze
It lifts its wheels above the ground,
It skims above the trees,
It rises high and higher
Away up toward the sun,
It's just a speck against the sky
---- And now it's gone!

Unknown

Remembrance Day

The following poem could be used as an introduction to this unit or it could be presented as a choral speaking piece during a Remembrance Day Ceremony at school.

Why Wear a Poppy?

"Please wear a poppy", the lady said.
And held one forth, but I shook my head.
Then I stopped and watched as she offered them there,
And her face was old and lined with care.
But beneath the scars the years had made
There remained a smile that refused to fade.

A boy came whistling down the street,
Bouncing along on care-free feet.
His smile was full of joy and fun.
"Lady", said he, "may I have one?"
When she pinned it on he turned to say,"Why do I wear a poppy today?"

The lady smiled in her wistful way,
And answered, "This is Remembrance Day."
And the poppy there is the symbol for the gallant men who died in war.
And because they did, you and I are free
That's why we wear a poppy, you see.

I had a boy about your size
With golden hair and big blue eyes.
He loved to play and jump and shout,
Free as a bird he would race about.
As the years went by he learned and grew,
And became a man --- as you will too

He was fine and strong, with a boyish smile
But he stayed with us such a little while
When war broke out and he went away,
I still remember his face that day,
When he smiled at me and said, "good-bye"
"I'll be back soon, Mom, please don't cry."

"But the war went on and he had to stay,
And all I could do is wait and pray.
His letters told of his terrible fight,
I can see it still in my dreams at night.
With the tanks and guns and cruel barbed wire.
And the mines and bullets, the bombs and fire."

"Till at last, the war was won ---
And that's why we wear a poppy, son."
The small boy turned as if to go,
Then said, "Thanks, lady, I'm glad to know.
That sure did sound like an awful fight,
But your son --- did he come back all right?"

A tear rolled down each faded cheek;
She shook her head, but didn't speak.
I slunk away in a sort of shame,
And if you were me you'd have done the same;
For thanks in giving, is oft delayed,
Though our freedom was bought --- and thousands paid!

And so when we see a poppy worn,
Let us reflect on the burden borne
By those who gave their very all!
When asked to answer their country's call
That we at home in peace might live.
Then wear a poppy! Remember and give.

Author Unknown

Music:

Teach songs about peace, Remembrance Day, friendship and freedom.

Examples: It Takes Time, Bridge Over Troubled Water, Blowin' in the Wind, Born Free. Some children may find it fun to learn songs that were sung during the war years. Make sure they know **O Canada** well. Teach them the **Maple Leaf Forever** and other Canadian Folk songs.

Art:

Involve your students in a poster contest. Discuss themes such as friendship, peace, freedom, war or Remembrance Day.

Wreaths could be made to hang on the classroom door or at home on the front door.

Drama:

Have your students learn to recite a Remembrance Day poem for a Remembrance Day Service at your school.

Guests:

Invite a war veteran or a member of your local Canadian Legion to speak to the class about Remembrance Day. Prepare questions in advance. Assign the questions to individual students to ask during the visit.

 # Remembrance Day

Displays:

Display books on Remembrance Day, the wars, war equipment and famous leaders around the room. On the bulletin board, post pictures of Remembrance Day ceremonies. Encourage your students to bring in memorabilia that their grandparents or their great grandparents collected during the war years such as medals, uniforms, black and white photographs. Display the items on a "Memories" table.

Mapping:

Obtain a large map of the world. Lay the map on a large table. Using modelling clay and a popsicle stick, make flags of the different countries involved in the wars. Place the flags on the countries.

Free Materials

All of the following materials are available free of charge to school libraries. Make your requests on school letterhead. The teacher-librarian should request the materials.

Write to: Public Affairs Division
Veterans Affairs Canada
Ottawa, Ontario
K1A 0P4

• **A Day of Remembrance** - Available in class sets (bilingual); Includes - Why remember?; What should we remember?; How do we remember?; Well illustrated with black and white photographs

• **Lieutenant Colonel John McCrae** - short, bilingual booklet on the author of "In Flanders Fields"; photograph of his grave; copy of his poem; history of the poppy as a symbol

• **The National War Memorial** - bilingual, well illustrated with photographs; explains the history of the memorial in Ottawa; explains the symbolism of the figures; comments of the sculptor; close-up photographs of the soldiers on the memorial

• **Valour Remembered: Canada and the Second World War** - bilingual; chapters on how the war began, Battle of the Atlantic, defence of Hong Kong, raid on Dieppe, conquest of Sicily, war at sea and in the air, liberation of the Netherlands, etc.; well illustrated with black and white photographs

• **Valour Remembered: Canada and the First World War** - similar to above with maps, chapters on the various battles at Vimy, The Somme, Passchendale, Hill 70, etc.

- **Valour Remembered: Canadians in Korea** - bilingual; includes maps, chapters on the background of the conflict; Canadian troops in action; various battles

- **Valour at Sea: Canada's Merchant Navy** - bilingual

- **Memorials to Canada's Dead** - bilingual; well illustrated; information on First World War Memorials in Europe and well known Canadian Memorials in Ottawa, Halifax, Victoria, etc.

- **Canada in the First World War and the Road to Vimy Ridge** - bilingual

- **Native Soldiers, Foreign Battlefields** - bilingual

There are also numerous posters on war themes.

Distributors:

The following list contains addresses of distributors from whom you may wish to order films, slides and other materials. There may be a small charge. Check before ordering.

- Canadian War Museum, 330 Sussex Drive, Ottawa, Ontario, K1A 0M8 Attention: Curator of War Art, Telephone: (613) 992-4330

- Modern Talking Pictures Service, Inc., 143 Sparks Avenue, Willowdale, Ontario, M2H 2S5, Telephone: (416) 498-7290

- National Film Board, 1 Lombard Street, Toronto, Ontario, M5C 2C1; Telephone: (416) 369-4094

- Ontario Educational Communications Authority (OECA), Canada Square, 2180 Yonge Street, Toronto, Ontario, M4S 2C1; Telephone: (416) 484-2700

- Ontario Provincial Command, Royal Canadian Legion, 218 Richmond Street West, Toronto, Ontario, M5V 1V8; Telephone: (416) 598-4466

- UNICEF Ontario, 101-38 Berwick Avenue, Toronto, Ontario, M5P 1H1; Telephone: (416) 487-4153

- United National Association in Canada, 808-63 Sparks Avenue, Ottawa, Ontario, K1P 5A6; Telephone: (613) 232-5751

 # Remembrance Day

Teacher Information

What is War?

War is a struggle that takes place when two large groups try to conquer or destroy each other. Since the beginning of time, there have been many kinds of wars. In early times, families fought families, tribes fought against tribes, and followers of one religion fought against followers of another. During modern times, wars have been fought between nations or groups of nations.

For hundreds of years, wars have been going on somewhere in the world nearly all the time. People hate wars because they always cause great hardship and suffering. In modern times, most nations or groups try to settle problems peacefully. Sometimes war results from a disagreement between nations, and sometimes from a desire for conquest.

In ancient times, people often fought so that they could get enough to eat. They would make war on neighbours in order to obtain new lands to grow food. During the 1600s through to the 1800s, this kind of war took place in North America between the pioneers and the Native People. The Native People wanted to roam freely over the land, hunting, trapping or fishing whereas the pioneers wanted to clear the land to plant their crops. Frequent wars and battles took place during this time period.

The people of ancient empires fought wars for wealth. The ruler of an empire and his or her advisors made the decision to conquer new lands for the purpose of collecting taxes from the people. They would hire armies to do their fighting. The people were not driven from their lands.

Alexander the Great led his soldiers against the Persian Empire in 334 B.C. The common people of the invaded lands paid little attention to the invasion. They only hoped their property would not be destroyed. They did not care which ruler collected the taxes.

Sometimes wars were fought by European nations to gain or increase their power. These wars united the people and strengthened the government.

Often countries feared the possibility of an attack and maintained armed forces to defend themselves. A country might fear a particular country and might choose its own time to strike the first blow. It might also choose to conquer some weaker neighbour to increase its own resources as a defense against attack.

There are usually various reasons and causes for a nation to make war against another nation. There are differences between the causes and reasons of a war. The government always states the "reasons" for the war in order to unite the people in the war effort. The "causes" of a war may be selfish, base, or even wicked while the reasons are usually lofty and noble.

World War I

World War I was originally called "The Great War" and it began in 1914 and ended in 1918. The assassination of Archduke Francis Ferdinand of Austria-Hungary in Sarajevo, the capital of Austri-Hungary's province of Bosnia-Herzegovina, sparked the outbreak of World War I. This was not the chief cause as many other factors had been developing in various countries during the 1800s. The main causes of World War I were the rise of nationalism, the build-up of military might, competition for colonies and a system of military alliances.

World War I began in the states of the Balkan Peninsula, the site of many small wars. This area in Europe has often been called "the powder keg of Europe". In the early 1900s, the Balkan States fought the Ottoman Empire in the First Balkan War (1912 - 1913) and again in the Second Balkan War (1913). The major power stayed out of the first two Balkan wars but they could not escape involvement during the third Balkan crisis.

Archduke Francis Ferdinand, heir to the throne of Austria-Hungary, decided to tour Bosnia-Herzegovina with his wife Sophie to ease tensions between the Balkans and Austria-Hungary. As the couple rode through Sarajevo on June 28, 1914, an assassin jumped onto their automobile and fired two shots. The Archduke and his wife died almost instantly. The assassin, Gavrilo Princip, was linked to a Serbian terrorist group called the "Black Hand".

This assassination gave Austria-Hungary an excuse to crush Serbia, its long time enemy in the Balkans.

Fighting Conditions During World War I

Before the Great War began, many countries were building strong armies and navies. Countries such as Germany and England were competing for seapower by building heavily armed modern battleships. Advances in technology and the techniques of industrialization increased the destructive power of military forces. Machine guns and other new arms that could fire more accurately and more rapidly were produced. Troops and supplies could move faster from place to place by steamships and railroads.

World War I was fought on land, in the air, and on the water. The airplane was first used in combat during World War I. These bombers held a pilot and a gunner and carried bombs under their wings. The tank was invented by the British. Tanks could rip through barbed wire and cross trenches. They held crews inside who gunned down enemies. The machine gun's rapid fire slaughtered many attacking infantrymen. It made World War I more deadly than earlier wars. The submarine was a warship that could fight under the water. It fired torpedoes that struck surface ships and then exploded.

Remembrance Day

Trench warfare took place during World War I. A system of trenches were dug by the opposing sides between France, Belgium and Germany. This was called the "Western Front". A "front-line" trench was 1.8 metres to 2.4 metres deep and was wide enough for two men to pass one another. Dugouts in the sides of the trenches protected the men during enemy fire. Barbed wire helped protect the front-line trenches from surprise attacks. Support trenches with field artillery were set up behind the front-line trenches.

Between the enemy lines lay a stretch of ground called "no man's land". This area could be from 2.7 metres wide at some points to more than 1.6 kilometres wide at others. Artillery fire tore up the area making it difficult to cross during an attack.

A soldier's life in the trenches was miserable and often very wet and uncomfortable. The smell of dead bodies hung in the air and rats caused constant problems. Time in the trenches would be filled with dull routines except during an attack. Soldiers took turns standing guard, repairing the trenches, kept phone wires in working order, brought food from behind the battle lines and at night repaired barbed wire and tried to find out information about the enemy.

The soldiers were pinned in the trenches by enemy artillery and machine guns. The Allies kept trying to break through the German lines. They would have the artillery bombard the enemy front-line trenches. The infantry then attacked as the commanders shouted "Over the top!". The soldiers scrambled quickly out of the trenches and began to run across "no man's land" with fixed bayonets. Grenades were thrown at the enemy trenches and the soldiers struggled to get through the barb wire. Unfortunately, the artillery failed to wipe out all resistance and enemy machine guns slaughtered wave after wave of advancing infantry.

The Allies and the Germans had developed new weapons which they hoped would help to break through these strong lines of defense. In April 1915, the Germans first released a poisonous gas over the Allied lines in the Second Battle of Ypres. The fumes from the gas caused vomiting and suffocation.

The Allies used a poisonous gas as well and gas masks became a necessary piece of equipment in the trenches. The flame thrower was another new weapon which shot out a stream of burning fuel.

Consequences of World War I

World War I left great destruction and many casualties. Nearly ten million soldiers died as a result of the war and about 21 million were wounded. The new weapons developed during this era, especially the machine gun, slaughtered many men. Germany, Russia and France lost the most servicemen.

Remembrance Day

Many important buildings, churches and homes were destroyed during the war. France and Belgium were hit the hardest. Armies destroyed farms and villages as they passed through them or dug trenches to fight battles. Factories, bridges and railroad tracks were wrecked by bombs and artillery shells.

Wars cost countries millions of dollars which they often had to borrow from wealthy countries. When the war was over, the countries were left in debt and it took a long time to pay the money back. Money was also needed to rebuild the country to its former state. Soldiers returning home did not have work as factories and businesses had been destroyed. Countries, in which the war had been fought, were left with heavy war debts, poor economies and no markets to ship their exports.

World War I changed the political climate in some of the countries. Four monarchies toppled after the war. Czar Nicholas II of Russia was the first monarch to lose his power in 1917. Kaiser Wilhelm II of Germany and Emperor Charles of Austria-Hungary left their thrones in 1918. The Ottoman Sultan, Mohammed VI lost his throne in 1922.

New countries were formed. The pre-war territory of Austria-Hungary formed the independent republics of Austria, Hungary and Czechoslovakia as well as parts of Italy, Poland, Romania and Yugoslavia. Russia and Germany gave up territory to Poland. Finland and the Baltic States of Estonia and Lithuania gained independence from Russia. World War I did give the Communists an opportunity to seize power in Russia.

World War I brought enormous changes to society in many of the countries. France lost many more young men than any of the other countries and its population dropped during the 1920s because of a low birth rate. Millions of people were uprooted during the war, losing everything they owned. Those who returned found their homes, villages and farms in ruins. Many people chose to make a living in urban areas instead of returning to their farms. Women found their independence during the war, holding down many jobs that men left to fight the war. They did not want to give up their new-found independence. Many countries had granted women the right to vote in elections after the war. European attitudes and ideals had been shattered, and they lost confidence and optimism in their way of life and culture.

World War II: 1939 - 1945

World War II involved 59 nations by the end of the war. It killed more people, destroyed more property, disrupted more lives, and had more far-reaching consequences than any other war in history. Historians feel that the unsolved problems felt by World War I and the treaties that ended it, created new political and economic problems.

Forceful dictators in Germany, Italy and Japan took advantage of these problems. They wanted to conquer additional territory to support their growing populations. After World War I,

treaties created hostile feelings leaving countries such as Italy and Japan dissatisfied, vowing to take action on their own. Countries such as Germany, Austria, Hungary, Bulgaria and Turkey were very unhappy as the treaties stripped them of territory and arms. They also had to make "reparations" (payments for war damages).

The economies of many European countries had been seriously damaged by the Great War. The victors were deeply in debt to the United States for war loans and the defeated countries found it difficult to pay for war damages to the victors. Many soldiers came home from World War I to find no work or jobs. The Great Depression which began in the United States in 1929 was felt worldwide. Europe's economic recovery was halted. The people suffered from mass unemployment, poverty and despair.

Nationalism was a chief cause of World War I and it grew even stronger after the war. Many Germans felt humiliated after their country's defeat in World War I and the harsh treatment under the peace treaties that their government had signed. They wished to see their country strong and powerful again. The people viewed foreigners and minority groups as inferior beings. During the 1930s many Germans supported a violent nationalistic organization called the "Nazi Party". Nationalism was also growing in strength in Italy and Japan.

The political unrest and poor economic conditions in European countries after World War II contributed to the rise of dictatorships in several countries. During the 1920s and 1930s, dictatorships came to power in the Soviet Union (Russia), Italy, Germany and Japan. These dictatorships held total power and ruled without regard for rules or laws. They used terror and secret police to crush any opposition to their rule. Those who objected or resisted were imprisoned or executed.

In the Soviet Union (Russia), Joseph Stalin became dictator in 1929. Benito Mussolini, leader of the Fascists, became dictator of Italy in 1922 when he and his group forced the king of Italy from his throne. Mussolini soon became known as "il duece" (the Leader). In 1933, Adolph Hitler, the leader of the Nazis, was appointed chancellor of Germany. Hitler became known as "der Fuhrer (the leader) and soon made Germany a dictatorship. He vowed to ignore the Treaty of Versailles, and promised to avenge Germany's defeat in World War I. Adolph Hitler wanted to have what he thought was a "superior race" and he preached that Jews and Slavs were inferior people. He led a campaign of hatred against the Jews and Communists, and promised the German people to rid the country of them.

In the 1930s, military officers began to hold office in Japan's government. Its military government glorified war and the training of warriors. In 1941, General Hideki Tojo became premier of Japan.

                                                                           SSC1-44

Japan, Italy and Germany invaded weak lands to expand their territories. In 1936, Germany and Italy agreed to support one another's foreign policies and formed the Rome-Berlin Axis. In 1940, Japan joined the alliance and it was then called the Rome-Berlin-Tokyo Axis. Japan's forces seized control of Manchuria, a region of China, rich in mineral resources. In 1937, Japan launched a major attack against China, Italy looked to Africa to fulfil its needs and ambitions for an empire. In 1936, Ethiopia was invaded by Italian troops. The use of machine guns, tanks, and airplanes soon overpowered Ethiopia's poorly equipped army. In Germany, Hitler was building up his armed forces in violation of the Treaty of Versailles. In March 1938, German troops marched into Austria and united it with Germany. On September 1,1939, Germany invaded Poland and began World War II. The Polish army was no match for Germany's new method of warfare called "blitzkrieg" or lightening war. The blitzkrieg stressed speed and surprise. Rows of tanks smashed through Poland's defences and were able to travel deep into Poland before the Polish army had time to react. German bombers and fighter aircraft knocked out communications and pounded battle lines.

On September 3, 1939, two days after the invasion of Poland, Britain and France declared war on Germany.

Consequences of World War II

World War II was a very destructive war. More lives were lost in this war than in any other one. Approximately seventeen million military people who served in the armed forces for the Allies and the Axis were killed. The Soviet Union (Russia) lost more people than any other country.

Many cities lay in ruins by the end of the war especially in Germany and Japan. Aerial bombing wrecked houses, factories, and transportation and communication systems. Millions of starving and homeless people wandered through the ruined cities and lands of Europe and Asia. Many civilians died during the war due to fires, diseases, and lack of health care. In the Soviet Union (Russia), nineteen million Soviet civilians died and in China, ten million died due to famine.

More than twelve million people who had been uprooted from their homes and country remained in Europe after the war. These people were called "displaced persons". They were orphans, prisoners of war, survivors of concentration camps or slave labour camps, and people who had fled invading armies and war-torn areas. Many had fled from countries in eastern Europe and refused to return to homelands that had come under communist rule.

Germany and Japan ended the war in complete defeat. Britain and France were severely weakened. The United States and the Soviet Union (Russia) emerged from the war as the world's leading powers. The Soviet Union wanted to spread "Communism" in Europe and Asia after the war. This brought about the "Cold War" between the United States and Russia.

The Soviet Union came out of the war much stronger than ever before. It had also absorbed the nations of Estonia, Latvia and Lithuania before the war ended and had taken parts of Poland, Romania, Finland and Czechoslovakia by 1945. A barrier known as the "iron curtain" divided eastern Europe from western Europe. Behind this invisible curtain, the Soviet Union helped Communist governments take power in Bulgaria, Czechoslovakia, Hungary, Poland, Romania and Korea.

The atomic bomb opened up the nuclear age and a race was on to develop nuclear weapons. Since then, people have feared their use.

The birth of the United Nations came out of the horror of World War II. This international organization agreed to work to promote peace. In April 1945, 50 nations gathered in San Francisco, California to draft and sign a charter for the United Nations.

The National War Memorial

The National War Memorial is located in Confederation Square in the city of Ottawa, Canada's capital city. This monument represents dignity, pride, courage, friendship and devotion to duty. It was erected to honour the 600 000 Canadian men and women who served and died for their country during World War I, but months after it was unveiled in 1939, World War II had begun. Today it commemorates 1.7 million wartime soldiers who have given their lives defending our country and its freedom.

Two carved figures which represent Peace and Freedom are situated above the large stone archway of the memorial. During the day, these figures appear triumphant and free against the bright, blue sky but in the dark of the night, they look remote and aloof and appear to suggest that Peace and Freedom are not to be taken lightly. All Canadians must work hard to attain these worthy gifts.

In the centre of the monument is a large group of 25 sculptured soldiers. Their rugged, virile forms illustrate the gallant efforts made by valiant, young Canadians during the war. The 25 soldiers are raised on a pedestal and they appear to be passing through the archway as if going forward to victory. The expression on the faces of the soldiers and the way they are grouped suggests a unit of purpose and a feeling of close comradeship.

The Remembrance Day Service at the War Memorial

World War I came to an end at eleven o'clock on November 11, 1918 -- the eleventh hour of the eleventh day of the eleventh month. The temporary peace document that was signed at the end of the war was called an armistice which come from the Latin word that means "arms (or weapons) stand still".

Remembrance Day

For many years in Canada, "Remembrance Day" was known as "Armistice Day". In 1933, the Canadian Parliament changed the name of the holiday to Remembrance Day and made November 11 a legal holiday. After World War II the day became a memorial day for those who died in both wars. There are still some veterans of World War II who march in Remembrance Day parades but there are very few people alive now who took part in World War I.

On November 11, in churches, in places of work, in schools or at war memorials, people all over the world attend services of Remembrance for those who died or for those who fought in the wars.

A solemn ceremony is held in Ottawa, at the National War Memorial in Confederation Square, to remember those who gave their lives for their country. Canadians from coast to coast are able to participate in this service through radio and television. The service is held in the morning. Veterans and representatives of the Armed Services parade around the base of the cenotaph. Bands play and choirs sing hymns of praise and thanksgiving. When the clock in the Peace Tower strikes eleven o'clock, it is a signal for the bugler to play the Last Post and the standard bearers to dip their Colours to the sound of the measured note.

A single gun shot begins the two-minute silence. The two-minute silence is ended by the bugler calling "Reveille". The Colours are raised, the bands play and the wreaths are placed on the cenotaph. The ceremony is ended with the bands playing and the spectators singing the National Anthem.

The Two Minute Silence

During any Remembrance Day Service, the most moving and significant experience is the time when we pause, bow our heads and remember those who made the supreme sacrifice in their fight against tyranny and oppression in order to safeguard the freedom and dignity of man. During these brief two minutes, be it at a service of remembrance in a school, in a church, in a factory, in an office, or at a cenotaph, we pay homage to the courage and devotion of the brave men and women who gave their lives in the service of their country. During this moment of reflection, the busy world is quiet, the noise of the traffic diminishes, the pace of the busy city slackens, and the voices of civilized men are still.

This period of silence resulted from a recommendation made after World War I by a South African statesman, Sir James Fitzpatrick. He is possibly better known to readers as the author of the adventure book entitled "Jock of the Bushveld". As a young man, Sir James spent some years in the exciting, adventurous and pioneer atmosphere of the gold-mining Witwatersrand. His later life was spent in the quieter setting of his South African farm. Fitzpatrick was a great lover of the wide open countryside and he spent a great deal of his time on the vast, stretching plains of his native land. The natural silence, away from the world of man, was conducive to thought and

reflection. Here the past again lived in the present and here he was inspired to make the plea that one of the finest tributes one could pay to the memory of one's comrades was to stand in silence and give one's thoughts to those who had lost their lives so that the free world might be a better place in which to live.

The Flowers of Remembrance

On Remembrance Day everyone wears a "poppy" as a reminder of the blood red flower that grew on the battlefields of France and Belgium where so many Canadians gave up their lives. During World War I much of the fighting was done in a place called Flanders. Every spring, the soldiers in the trenches noticed that poppies grew over the graves of their friends who were killed.

When the war ended and the soldiers came home, they still remembered their comrades who were buried in Flanders. When they thought of the graves, they remembered the poppies that grew around the graves. The men who returned from the war decided they would wear a poppy each year to show that they still remembered their friends.

On November 11 in 1918, the First World War ended. The men who had been in the war picked that day each year to wear a poppy. Even people who had not been involved in the war, but who had loved the soldiers who did not return, also wore a poppy to show that they remembered the dead.

Wreaths made of poppies entwined with oak and maple leaves are placed on war memorials all across Canada on November 11 every year. A wreath is placed on the National War Memorial in Ottawa by a woman who has been chosen to represent all mothers of sons or daughters who have given their life during military service.

Real poppies are hard to obtain and there were not enough to go around. Men who had been badly wounded during World War I and who could not work at other jobs began to make poppies out of cloth. The early poppies were red cloth petals with black centres. This cloth poppy symbolized the real flower which grew over the graves of the men who died during World War I.

For many tears after the war, children stood in silence with their parents on Remembrance Day. They all wore a poppy, stood quietly, and remembered the men who had been killed during the war. When these same children grew up there was another war. The boys who were then young men went to fight in Word War II. Many of these young men were sent to the same places as the men they had stood silently for and remembered. Many of these young men died in the same places.

When World War II ended more people than ever wanted to wear a poppy. There were more men than ever to remember and honour. There were sailors and airmen as well as soldiers. These men died to protect the people who lived in Canada and those who would be born in the future.

The men who fought and died in the war wanted us to enjoy all the good things in life. They wanted our homes to be safe and they wanted us to have the opportunity to go to the school and the church of our choice.

On Remembrance Day, when everyone wears a poppy and stands in silence, we are saying "thank you" to all those who died for us and our country.

The Peace Tower

The "Peace Tower" was built to honour the sacrifices of 66 657 Canadian soldiers who laid down their lives in the cause of peace during World War I. It is the focal point of Parliament Hill and is known as one of the finest Gothic structures in the world. It is perhaps the most admired and revered part of Parliament Hill. National Memorials, The Memorial Chamber, The Book of Remembrance and the Carillon of Bells are its treasured contents. The Peace Tower stands 90.6 metres high and a lookout is found at the top where magnificent views of Ottawa can be seen. There is also a four-faced clock that measures 4.8 metres in diameter.

The Carillon of Bells consists of 53 bells of varying sizes. The largest bell weighs 10 080 kilogrammes. The smallest bell weighs 4.5 kilogrammes. The beautiful instrument is played from a wooden keyboard fashioned after the 300 year old Flemish system. Musicians have come from all over the world to study the magnificently tuned Carillon.

The Memorial Chamber was dedicated as a memorial to Canadians who were in the First World War. It was officially opened November 11th, 1928 by Rt. Honourable William Lyon Mackenzie King, then Prime Minister. The walls and ceilings are made of a special stone that was a gift from the people of France. The border of black marble and the altar steps came from the people of Belgium. The floor is comprised of stone gathered from the various areas in which Canadian soldiers served. Inlaid brass plates denote the principal battles Canadians fought in such as Ypres, Mount Sorrel, Somme, Vimy Ridge, Hill 70, Passchendaele, Amiens, Arras, Cambrai, Valenciennes and Mons.

The walls of the Memorial Chamber hold carved marble panels that tell the Canadian story during the war to end all wars. Each panel illustrates the sacrifices and achievements of the Canadian Armed Forces during World War I.

 # Remembrance Day

Within the Memorial Chamber is found the Altar of Sacrifice. It holds the Book of Remembrance in a gold frame decorated with the Royal Arms and the Arms of Canada. The name of each Canadian soldier who gave his life in the service of his country appears in the Book. The pages are turned according to a calendar so that each is on view the same day of the same month in each year.

The Books of Remembrance of World War II, the Korean War, South African War and the Nile Expedition are also found within the Memorial Chamber.

Famous Canadian War Heroes

During the First and Second World Wars, countless men and women fought and many died defending Canada. Many of our young Canadian men performed heroic and daring deeds in the throes of battle. Read about the adventures of some of our famous Canadian War Heroes.

Billy Barker

Billy Barker was born in 1894 in Dauphin, Manitoba. He was one of the greatest fighter pilots of World War I. Billy Barker shot down 53 enemy aircraft during the war. He was known for the different methods that he used while shooting down the enemy. His tactics were quite different than other pilots. Billy flew a plane called the Sopwith Camel. This type of plane was quite agile at low altitudes and manoeuvred well in a limited air space.

Billy would lure the enemy down to his level by flying close to the ground instead of diving on his enemy from above. His ability to manoeuvre his Sopwith Camel easily at low altitudes was an advantage over the faster German planes.

During the war, Billy Barker and his Squadron attacked many air bases in northern Italy, and they virtually grounded the Austrian air force. In the last month of the war, he performed his most outstanding feat. On a flight to England, all by himself, he took on 60 enemy aircraft. He succeeded in downing five of the enemy aircrafts before he went crashing to the ground. He amazingly survived the crash and was awarded the Victoria Cross for his incredible air battle.

In 1930, after the war, Billy Barker died when the airplane that he was flying crashed at Rockcliffe Air Station in Ottawa.

Buzz Beurling

Buzz Beurling was born in 1921 in Verdun, Quebec. He was one of the most outstanding pilots during World War II. At the age of fourteen, he flew his first plane and at seventeen, he won an aerobatic competition. Unfortunately, because he lacked education, he could not join the Royal Canadian Air Force.

Buzz wanted to participate in the war effort and applied to the Royal Air Force in Britain. He was accepted by Britain and became one of their star pilots. In 1942, he played an important part in the successful defence of the Island of Malta. While helping to defend Malta from the German and Italian forces, he shot down 27 enemy aircraft in less than five months.

Buzz transferred to the Royal Canadian Air Force because he had achieved fame for his efforts defending Malta. Unfortunately he was not happy in the Canadian Air Force. Buzz was very much a loner and he was better at making decisions than at taking orders. He resigned from the Royal Canadian Air Force in 1944.

Four years later, he decided to help Israel fight its war against the Arabs. Regrettably, he died on the way to Israel when his plane caught fire over an airfield outside of Rome, Italy.

Billy Bishop

Billy Bishop was born in Owen Sound, Ontario in 1894. He was one of the most famous air aces of World War I. He became famous for his phenomenal record of having shot down 72 enemy planes.

Billy often went out alone, and would fly far behind enemy lines. He would make surprise attacks on German air bases. His type of courage was considered the most difficult kind, "the courage of the early morning". He was awarded the Victoria Cross as well as other medals for his bravery and incredible feats.

After the war, Billy married Timothy Eaton's granddaughter and became a successful businessman. For a while, he ran a small aviation business with his partner, Billy Barker, who was also a war hero. Later he became an oil executive. During the Second World War, he was an honourary Air Marshall and was in charge of recruiting young people into the Airforce, and helping to boost the war effort.

A. Roy Brown

A. Roy Brown was born in Carleton Place, Ontario in 1893. He was a fighter pilot during World War I. During the war, he was the famous pilot who shot down Germany's greatest air ace, the famous "Red Baron", Manfred von Richthofen.

On the day this exciting event took place, a young inexperienced Canadian pilot named Wop May was on his first combat fight. The famous Red Baron was right behind Wop May, pursuing him. A. Roy Brown saw what was going to happen and began firing at the Red Baron's plane. At the same time, the Australian gunners were firing from the ground. They also hit the Red Baron's plane, and just who was responsible for shooting down the Red Baron's planes was disputed for a long time. A. Roy Brown was certain he had, but it now seems likely that it was an Australian bullet that actually killed the Red Baron.

Remembrance Day

During the war, A. Roy Brown was suffering from battle fatigue and actually fainted while flying his plane causing it to crash. He pulled through and survived the crash, even though he was not expected to live. After the war he went into his own air service business.

Andrew Mynarski

Pilot Officer Andrew Mynarski was born in Winnipeg, Manitoba in 1916. He is considered the most heroic of all the Canadian war heroes. One day, while on a mission, his plane was attacked and caught on fire. He ordered all of his crew to bail out of the blazing aircraft. Unfortunately, the rear gunner couldn't as he was trapped in his turret. Mynarski fought through the flames and tried to free the gunner. It was a fruitless effort and the gunner insisted that he at least save himself. Mynarski went back through the flames to the escape hatch.

As a last effort to encourage the trapped gunner, Mynarski stood at attention and saluted the gunner, even though his parachute and clothes were on fire. Then he jumped to safety. Mynarski was very badly burned and later died of his injuries. The gunner surprisingly survived the crash and lived to tell of the pilot's amazing courage. In 1944, Mynarski was awarded a posthumous Victoria Cross.

John McCrae

John McCrae was born in Guelph, Ontario in 1872. He was the second of three sons. His father, Captain David McCrae who commanded the Ontario Field Battery, owned a woollen mill in Guelph.

John attended the University of Guelph and became a doctor. During his university days, he like to write poetry and several of his poems were published in magazines and newspapers.

In 1899, he enlisted as a lieutenant in the Canadian Field Artillery for duty in the South African or Boer War. When the war ended, he returned to being a doctor and to writing poetry.

When World I began he joined the First Canadian Contingent. He became a major and First Brigade Artillery surgeon, and was stationed in Flanders during the spring of 1915. His medical station was located on the banks of the Ypres Canal near the village of Ypres.

On May 2, 1915, one of John McCrae's close friends, Alexis Helmer, was killed during the Second Battle of Ypres. The next morning one of his friends, Sergeant-Major Allinson, saw him sitting on the step of an ambulance writing on a pad of paper. Sergeant-Major Allinson noticed that his face was calm but tired, and that his eyes frequently strayed to Helmer's grave. The poem that he wrote was an exact description of the scene in front of him. Larks were really flying overhead, while artillery boomed at the front and poppies fluttered in the breeze between the crosses. The poem that he had written was called "In Flanders Fields". This poem made John McCrae famous throughout the world.

John McCrae was killed by the war but not by a bullet or shell. The time that he had spent fighting in the Boer War in Africa and in the First World War broke down his health, and he died of pneumonia and meningitis on January 28, 1918.

His uniforms and personal effects went down in a ship that was torpedoed. However, many of his letters, newspaper clippings and other memorabilia are found at his home in Guelph. John McCrae's home is a museum, and open to the public.

Tomb of the Unknown Soldier

On May 23, 2000, a Canadian Forces aircraft flew to France to bring the Unknown Soldier back to Canada. On the evening of May 25, the casket, carrying the remains of the Unknown Soldier, was taken to the Parliament Buildings where it lay in state in the Hall of Honour for three days. Canadians were allowed to view the casket and pay their respects.

In May 28th, the Unknown Soldier was taken to Parliament Hill to the National War Memorial on a horse-drawn gun carriage provided by the Royal Canadian Mounted Police. The coffin was laid to rest in a specially designed sarcophagus directly in front of the War Memorial.

The Tomb of the Unknown Soldier honours more than 116 000 Canadians who have sacrificed their lives in the cause of peace and freedom. It will be the focal point of commemoration for all memorial events at the National War Memorial

Remembrance Day Activities

The following activities may be used in any manner or order that the teacher wishes. They cover a wide grade-level span in the following subjects: Phonics, Word Study, Reading and Creative Writing. The sheets may be completed as a large group activity or placed at an interest centre on Remembrance Day.

The Creative Writing Activities and the Follow-up Booklet are opened-ended so the teacher may adjust the amount of information written by the students at each grade level. Lines have been provided for each picture. The number of pages produced on the topic of Remembrance Day for the booklet is to be determined by the teacher and the grade level of the students using it.

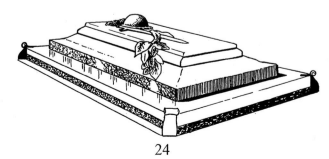

Pp Poppy

Colour all the pictures that start like "poppy" **red**.

How does it begin?

In each box is a **Remembrance Day** picture.
On the line **print** the sound that each picture begins with.

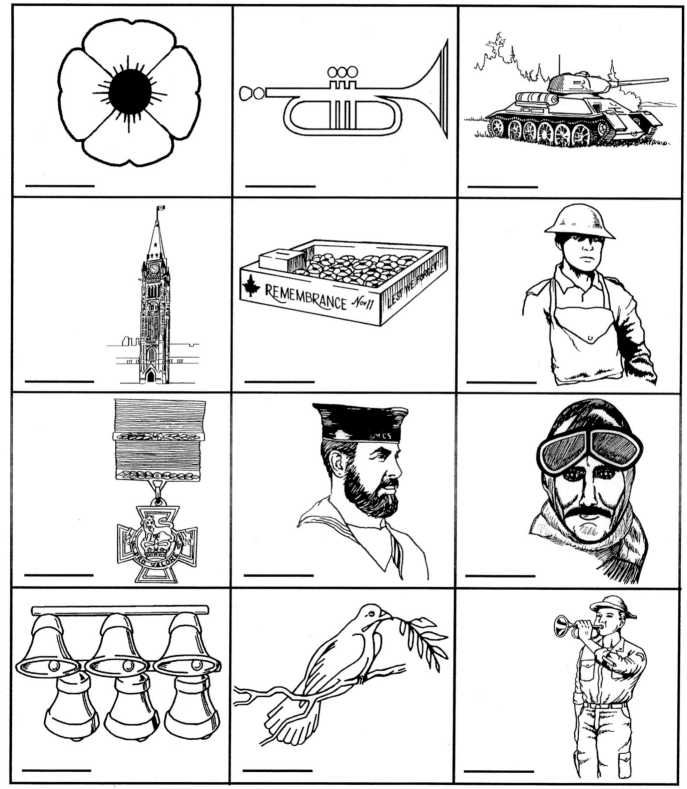

Skill: Recognition of the "Cr" Blend

White **crosses** were used to mark the
graves of soldiers who died in the wars.

Cr   Crosses

The word **"crosses"** begins with the blend **"cr"**.

Circle the pictures that begin with the same sound.

On Remembrance Day a **wreath** is placed on the war monument.

In the word **wreath** we can hear the **long vowel e** sound.

Colour each box **green** that has a word with a **long** vowel sound.

war	peace	bugle
tower	sailor	brave
pilot	cross	hero
silence	soldiers	sing
mark	march	grave
field	pray	bands
bells	praise	troops

Listen for the Vowel Sound

The **poppy** is a bright red flower.

In the word **poppy** we can hear the short vowel "**o**" sound.

Colour each poppy **red** that has a word with a **short** vowel sound.

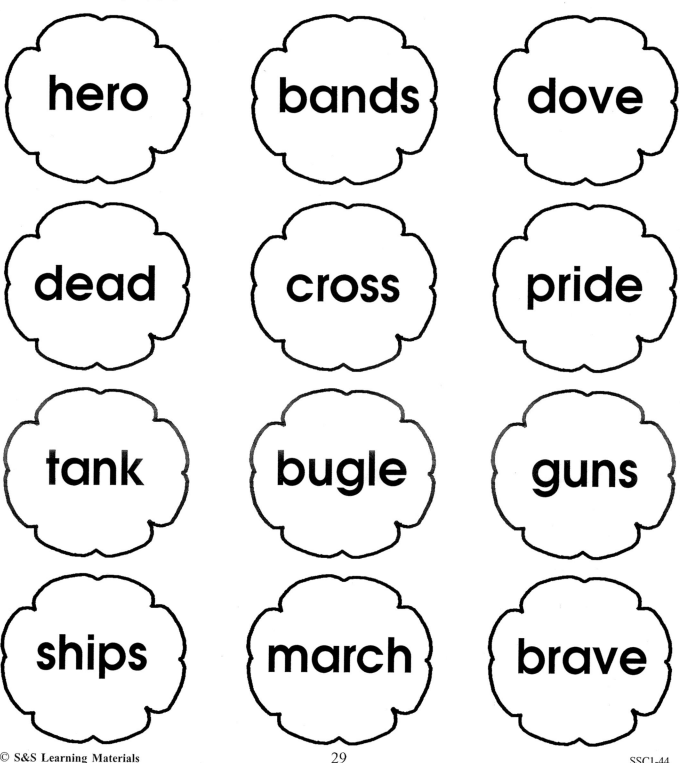

Does it begin with "Fl" or "F"?

Many soldiers were buried in **Flanders Fields**.

The name **Flanders Fields** begins with **"fl"**.

Does the picture begin with **"f"** or **"fl"**?

Print the correct sound on the line in each box.

Mm is for Monument

A monument is a large stone structure found in a park or special square in a city or town.

It is built to remember people who have fought and died for their country.

The word **monument** begins with the sound that **"m"** makes.

Colour the pictures in the boxes that begin like monument **yellow**.

Does it begin with "s", "sl", or "sh" ?

Many Canadian sailors travelled on war **ships** to countries in Europe.

The word **ship** begins with the sound that **"sh"** makes.

Print the correct sound that each picture begins with on the line in each box.

Does it begin with "pl", "pr" or "p"?

Many young airmen flew **planes** during the war.

The word **plane** begins with the blend **"pl"**.

Circle the correct sound that each picture begins with.

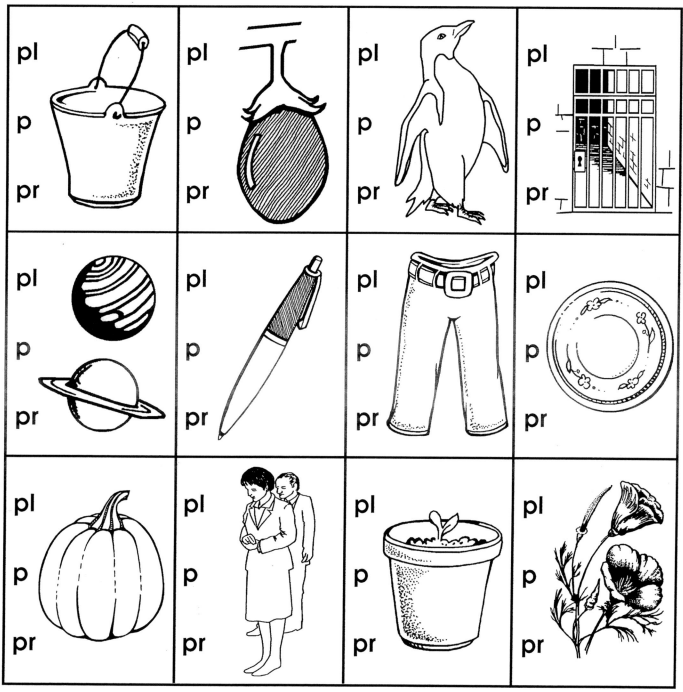

Does it begin with "d", "b", "c" or "p"?

The **dove** is a gentle bird and is a symbol of peace.

The word **dove** begins with the sound that "d" makes

Circle the correct sound that each picture begins with.

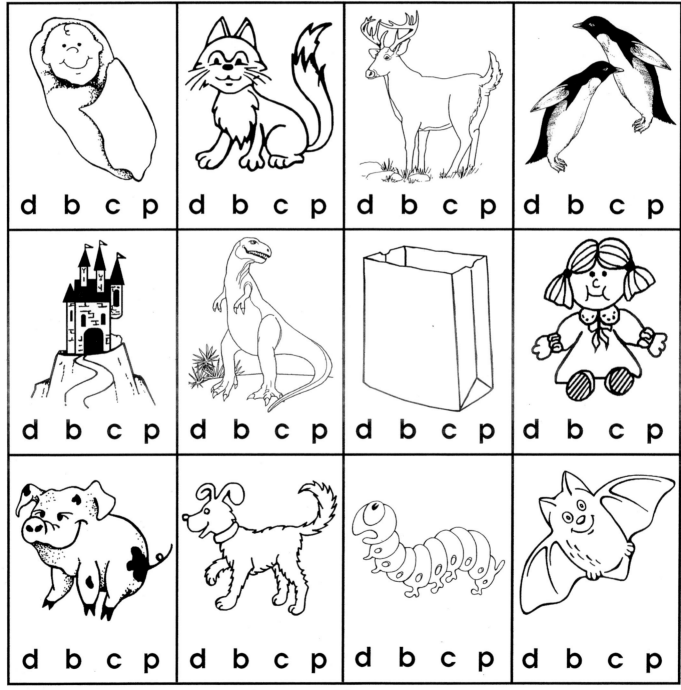

Skill: Matching Word Card to Picture Card

Cut out the picture cards and word cards. Mount them on a sturdy backing and laminate. Store the cards in an envelope. Attach the instruction card to the envelope. Place at a centre on Remembrance Day.

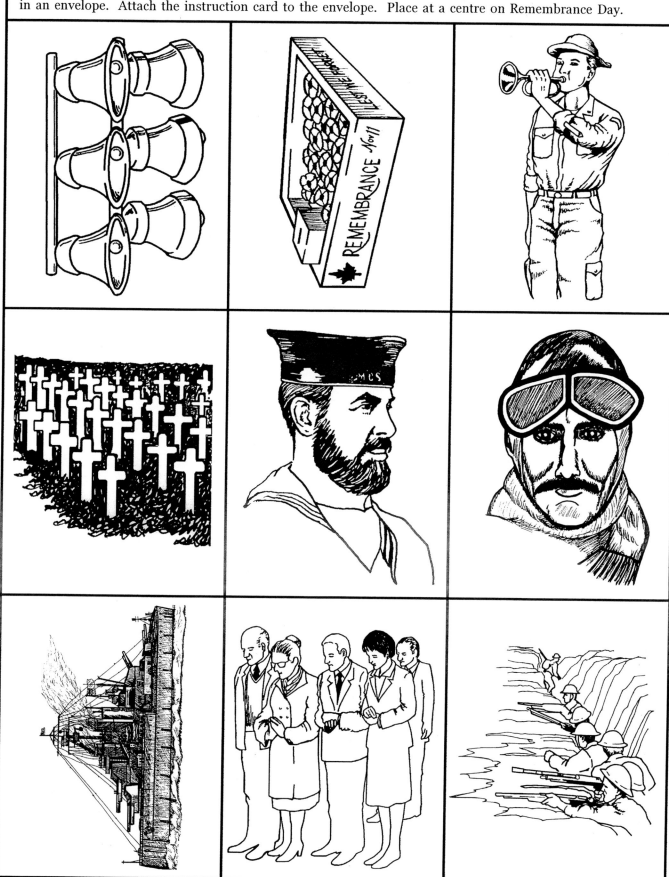

Cut out the picture cards and word cards. Mount them on a sturdy backing and laminate. Store the cards in an envelope. Attach the instruction card to the envelope. Place at a centre on Remembrance Day.

Cut out the picture cards and word cards. Mount them on a sturdy backing and laminate. Store the cards in an envelope. Attach the instruction card to the envelope. Place at a centre on Remembrance Day.

poppy	**wreath**
tank	**medal**
veteran	**doves**
monument	**bells**
plane	**poppy box**
soldier	**bugler**

Cut out the picture cards and word cards. Mount them on a sturdy backing and laminate. Store the cards in an envelope. Attach the instruction card to the envelope. Place at a centre on Remembrance Day.

cross	**sailor**
pilot	**war ship**
pray	**trench**

Attach the instruction card to the envelope

Remembrance Day Matching

Match the picture card and the word card.

Example:

poppy

Skill: Identifying the Number of Syllables in Words

Working With Words

Each year on November 11, wreaths are placed at a monument.

The word **monument** has **three** syllables or word parts.

On the chart, **print** the words in the poppies in the correct syllable box.

One Syllable	Two Syllables	Three Syllables

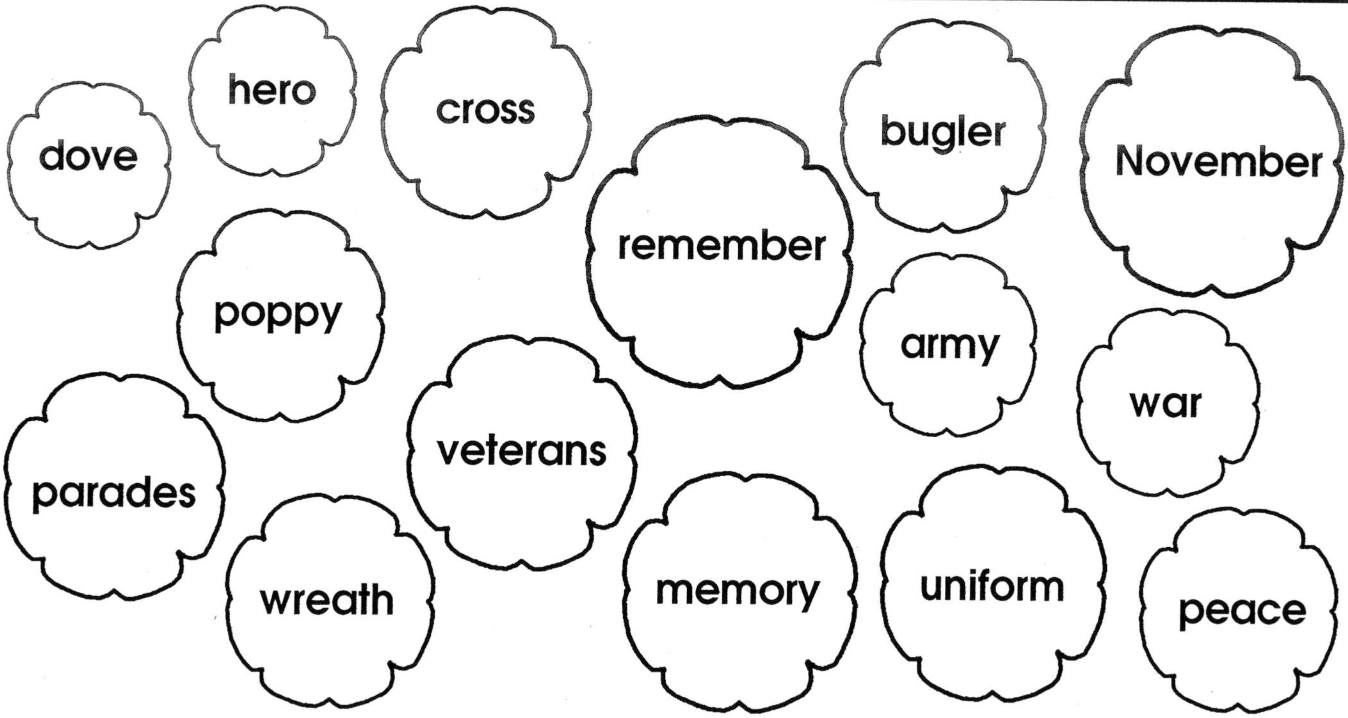

dove
hero
cross
remember
bugler
November
poppy
army
war
parades
veterans
wreath
memory
uniform
peace

Working With Words

On November 11, Remembrance Day takes place in every city and town in Canada.

There are words that we use and think of on that day.

Look for the Remembrance Day words in the word search.

Circle each one.

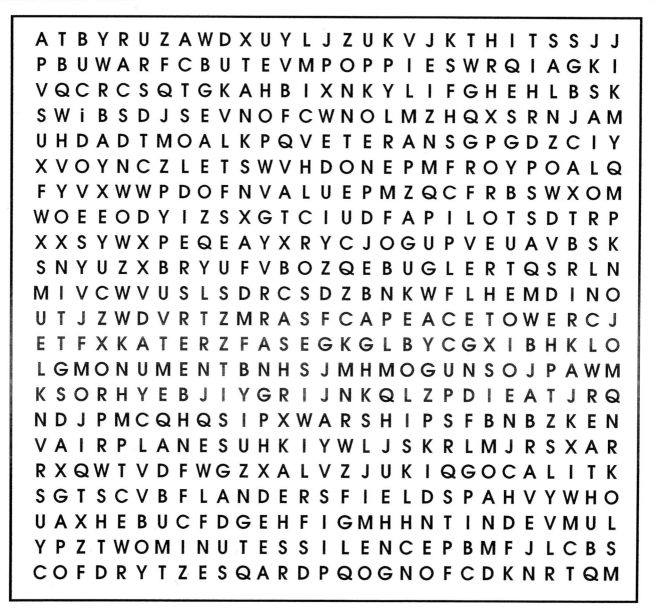

```
A T B Y R U Z A W D X U Y L J Z U K V J K T H I T S S J J
P B U W A R F C B U T E V M P O P P I E S W R Q I A G K I
V Q C R C S Q T G K A H B I X N K Y L I F G H E H L B S K
S W i B S D J S E V N O F C W N O L M Z H Q X S R N J A M
U H D A D T M O A L K P Q V E T E R A N S G P G D Z C I Y
X V O Y N C Z L E T S W V H D O N E P M F R O Y P O A L Q
F Y V X W W P D O F N V A L U E P M Z Q C F R B S W X O M
W O E E O D Y I Z S X G T C I U D F A P I L O T S D T R P
X X S Y W X P E Q E A Y X R Y C J O G U P V E U A V B S K
S N Y U Z X B R Y U F V B O Z Q E B U G L E R T Q S R L N
M I V C W V U S L S D R C S D Z B N K W F L H E M D I N O
U T J Z W D V R T Z M R A S F C A P E A C E T O W E R C J
E T F X K A T E R Z F A S E G K G L B Y C G X I B H K L O
L G M O N U M E N T B N H S J M H M O G U N S O J P A W M
K S O R H Y E B J I Y G R I J N K Q L Z P D I E A T J R Q
N D J P M C Q H Q S I P X W A R S H I P S F B N B Z K E N
V A I R P L A N E S U H K I Y W L J S K R L M J R S X A R
R X Q W T V D F W G Z X A L V Z J U K I Q G O C A L I T K
S G T S C V B F L A N D E R S F I E L D S P A H V Y W H O
U A X H E B U C F D G E H F I G M H H N T I N D E V M U L
Y P Z T W O M I N U T E S S I L E N C E P B M F J L C B S
C O F D R Y T Z E S Q A R D P Q O G N O F C D K N R T Q M
```

I found _____ Remembrance Day words

SSC1-44

Skill: Using Antonyms in Sentences

Working With Antonyms

Many men and women lost their lives during the two World Wars.

The words **"men"** and **"women"** are **antonyms** or opposites.

Use each pair of antonyms in the brackets in each sentence correctly.

1. Let us always _____ the men who gave their lives and never _____ their bravery. **(forget, remember)**

2. Many brave men and women had to _____ so that you can _____ in a peaceful country. **(die, live)**

3. Canada is a country where there is _____ and no _____. **(war, peace)**

4. Many _____ soldiers felt _____ while they stood in the trenches fighting the enemy. **(afraid, brave)**

5. It takes years to _____ beautiful buildings while bombs can _____ them in minutes. **(build, destroy)**

6. The _____ streets of many cities and towns across Canada become _____ during the Two-Minutes of Silence on Remembrance Day. **(noisy, silent)**

7. _____ children and _____ veterans stand silently together and pray for the dead soldiers in front of the cenotaph on Remembrance Day. **(old, young)**

8. Wars can cause countries who were at one time _____ to become _____. **(friends, enemies)**

9. During the two world wars many battles were _____ but many lives were _____. **(won, lost)**

10. During the wars many Canadian _____ became soldiers while the _____ worked in factories. **(men, women)**

Working With Synonyms

In the box are words that are **synonyms** to the underlined words in the sentences. On the line provided at the end of each sentence, **print** the synonym for the **underlined** word.

W.W. 2	songs	graveyard	costumes
soldier	mean	hurt	troops
quietly	cenotaph	airmen	friends

1. At the Remembrance Day Service choirs sing <u>hymns</u> while bands play. _____

2. Adolph Hitler was a <u>cruel</u> leader who caused much harm to the Jewish people during the World War II. _____

3. The group of people at the cenotaph stood <u>silently</u> for two minutes. _____

4. In the <u>cemetery</u> in Flanders Fields, rows of white crosses mark the graves of many dead soldiers. _____

5. Many soldiers were <u>wounded</u> during the battles and had to be sent home. _____

6. Wreaths were placed at our city's <u>monument</u>. _____

7. Many <u>soldiers</u> fought from trenches that were wet and uncomfortable. _____

8. Pilots flew planes that carried bombs under their wings and a gunner during World War I. _____

9. Veterans of the two World Wars lost many <u>comrades</u>. _____

10. Sailors, soldiers and airmen wore different <u>uniforms</u>. _____

Working With Homonyms

The words **"war"** and **"wore"** are homonyms.

Homonyms are words that sound the same but are not spelled the same way and have different meanings.

Under each sentence is a pair of homonyms. **Choose** the correct homonym that fits each sentence. **Print** it on the line.

1. Billy Bishop flew an airplane during World _____ I.
   (**wore, war**)

2. Soldiers, sailors and airmen _____ uniforms. (**where, wear**)

3. The _____ Tower was built in Ottawa to honour Canadian soldiers. (**Piece, Peace**)

4. The old woman placed a wreath on the monument in memory of her dead _____. (**sun, son**)

5. All the men buried in Flanders Fields _____ during the world wars. (**dyed, died**)

6. Sailors travelled in submarines deep in the _____. (**see, sea**)

7. The army captain _____ his men carefully through the forest. (**lead, led**)

8. Billy Barker, a war ace, flew a _____ called a Sopwith Camel. (**plain, plane**)

9. The soldiers hid in the old barn for about a _____ before they were rescued. (**weak, week**)

10. On Remembrance Day we _____, bow our heads and remember those who died during the wars. (**paws, pause**)

43   SSCI-44

Working With Rhyming Words

The words **"hero"** and **"zero"** rhyme.

Underline the words in each group that **rhyme.**

1.	sailor	cross	fight	boss	navy	toss
2.	peace	fight	light	army	right	red
3.	brave	dead	grave	hero	save	bugle
4.	dove	died	glove	guns	bands	love
5.	tank	bank	sank	silent	choirs	thank
6.	tower	sailor	pilots	tailor	deed	trailor
7.	shout	shoot	hoot	dove	boot	bands
8.	ship	navy	cross	wavy	cross	gravy
9.	band	sand	hand	land	lost	hat
10.	bells	shells	shop	poppy	smells	swells

44   SSC1-44

LEST WE FORGET

Complete the crossword puzzle carefully.

LEST WE FORGET

Crossword Puzzle Clues

Across

1. The place were many soldiers are buried.
2. He plays the Last Post on Remembrance Day.
3. a large group of soldiers
4. They mark the graves in Flanders Fields.
5. It is a bright red flower.
6. The song played by the bugler.
7. the eleventh month of the year
8. the colour of a poppy
9. It is made of poppies and oak leaves.

Down

1. men who fly planes
2. a symbol of peace
3. It is held on November 11.
4. A time when there is no noise.
5. Men who fight during wars.
6. People who have fought in wars.

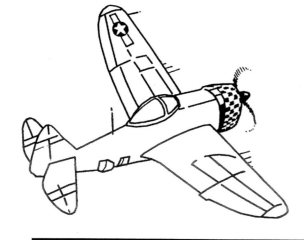

Puzzle Words

Flanders Fields	silence	airmen
Remembrance Day	dove	crosses
veterans	army	wreath
Last Post	red	poppy
November	soldiers	bugler

Working With Plurals

A word that means only one is a **singular** word. **Example:** pilot

A word that means more than one is a **plural** word. **Example:** pilots

Print the **singular** or **plural** form of the word on the line in each sentence.

1. (**Poppy, Poppies**) _____ are red flowers that grew on the graves of soldiers in Flanders Fields.

2. (**Army, Armies**) _____ from many different countries fought in both world wars.

3. (**woman, women**) A _____ who has lost a son or daughter in a war is chosen to place a wreath on the cenotaph.

4. (**soldier, soldiers**) The _____ bowed his head and said a prayer for his dead friends.

5. (**trench, trenches**) The soldiers in World War I spent most of their time fighting in _____.

6. (**Veteran, Veterans**) _____ sell poppies to people to wear on Remembrance Day.

7. (**cross, crosses**) John McCrae wrote about the rows of _____ in Flanders Fields in his poem.

8. (**Cemetery, Cemeteries**) _____ all over the world have the graves of dead soldiers.

9. (**torpedo, torpedoes**) Submarines use _____ to destroy enemy ships.

10. (**hero, heroes**) Andrew Mynarski, a Canadian pilot, is one of Canada's war _____.

Remembrance Day Sentences

The sentences below are all mixed up.

Write the words in the **correct order** on the lines provided.

1. shot down / 72 / Billy Bishop / enemy planes.

   _____

   _____

2. in Flanders Fields. / wrote / John McCrae / the poem

   _____

   _____

3. sell poppies / for Remembrance Day. / War veterans

   _____

   _____

4. is held / Remembrance Day / on November eleventh

   _____

   _____

5. in Flanders Fields. / Poppies are / that grow / bright red flowers

   _____

   _____

6. plays / the Last Post / The bugler / at eleven o'clock.

   _____

   _____

Remembrance Day Thoughts

Take some time and think of a good ending for each sentence beginning.

1. Soldiers are sent to fight wars because _____

_____

_____

2. I am thankful that Canada is a peaceful country because _____

_____

_____

3. I think Remembrance Day is important because _____

_____

_____

4. People should buy poppies because _____

_____

_____

5. Countries should not go to war because _____

_____

_____

6. We should think of men and women who died in the wars because

_____

_____

_____

I am proud of Canada because ....

Being proud of something that you have or something that you have done is important.

Complete each sentence below telling why you are proud.

1. I am proud of my country, Canada, because _____

   _____

   _____

2. Canada's flag makes me feel proud because _____

   _____

   _____

3. I am proud to be a Canadian because _____

   _____

   _____

4. I am proud of Canada's war veterans because _____

   _____

   _____

5. I am proud when I sing "O Canada" because _____

   _____

   _____

6. I am proud of Canada's soldiers, sailors and pilots because _____

   _____

   _____

7. I am proud of new Canadians because _____

   _____

   _____

Buying a Poppy

It was a cool November day. A little boy _____

_____

_____

_____

_____

_____

_____

_____

_____

_____

_____

Fighting in the Trenches

All day long I stood in the damp trench waiting for something to happen.

Suddenly _____

_____

_____

_____

_____

_____

_____

_____

_____

_____

52

Remembrance Day

It was Remembrance Day. The choir was singing a sad song. Everyone

was_____

_____

_____

_____

_____

_____

_____

_____

_____

_____

_____

_____

The Enemy is Coming!

We knew it was time to leave. Our town was being attacked. We could

hear _____

_____

_____

_____

_____

_____

_____

_____

_____

_____

_____

_____

Getting Along

Unrest in the world is often caused because countries cannot get along.

There are times when children do not get along.

Put a check mark on the line beside each reason that causes children not to get along.

____ pushing in line

____ sharing toys with others

____ being friendly

____ telling on someone

____ not sharing things

____ playing a mean trick on someone

____ inviting someone to a party

____ saying something nice to someone

____ calling someone names

____ hitting someone

____ tripping someone

____ making someone cry

____ pulling someone's hair

____ giving a friend a hug

____ making fun of someone's clothes

____ inviting a new classmate to play a game

____ making fun on someone's looks

____ helping a classmate

____ breaking someone's toy

____ saying mean things about someone

____ telling lies

____ giving things to someone poor

____ yelling angrily at your friends

____ sharing your lunch

SSC1-44

After the War

Wars leave countries and the people in a very bad way.

Put a check mark on the line beside each sentence that describes the way a war hurts people and a country.

___ 1. Very few people get hurt during a war.

___ 2. Many important buildings such as churches, museums and palaces are destroyed during a war.

___ 3. Countries are richer and have lots of money after a war.

___ 4. Many people are killed during the war.

___ 5. There are plenty of jobs for soldiers when they returned home after the war.

___ 6. Many people lose their homes and all of their things.

___ 7. There is much peace and happiness at the end of a war.

___ 8. Wars make people feel ashamed and unhappy.

___ 9. People are richer after the war and live in beautiful homes.

___10. Countries are in debt and owe much money to other countries.

___11. Cities look the same after the war.

___12. People return home to find their homes, villages and farms in ruins.

___13. Factories, bridges and railroad tracks are wrecked by bombs.

___14. Countries become smaller because they have to give land away after the war.

Remembrance Day Reading

The Poppy

Everyone wears a poppy on Remembrance Day. It reminds us to think about the soldiers who died during the wars.

During World War I, many battles were fought in a place called Flanders. Many dead soldiers were buried in a cemetery called Flanders Fields. On the graves grew a red flower called a poppy. The men who returned to Canada from the war remembered the red flower that grew in the cemetery. They decided to wear a poppy to show they were thinking of their dead friends on November 11.

In time, real poppies were hard to find. Men who had been badly wounded during the war began to make them out of cloth. These poppies had red cloth petals with black centres. Today, the poppy is made out of cloth and plastic. War veterans sell them before Remembrance Day.

Print **Yes** or **No** on the line after each sentence.

1. Red roses are worn on Remembrance Day. _____

2. The poppy grew on the graves of soldiers in Flanders Fields. _____

3. Real poppies were worn at first on Novemebr 11. _____

4. Cloth poppies were made in factories for Remembrance Day. _____

5. Poppies worn today are bright red with yellow centres. _____

6. War veterans sell poppies before Remembrance Day. _____

7. Poppies were worn on Remembrance Day because they were a pretty flower. _____

8. The poppy worn today is bright red with a black centre. _____

Remembrance Day Reading

The National War Memorial

The National War Memorial is found in Confederation Square in Ottawa, Canada's capital city. It was built in memory of all the Canadian men and women who served and died for their country.

The monument is a large stone archway. At the top of the archway stands two carved figures that represent peace and freedom. In the centre of the archway is a large group of 25 carved soldiers. The soldiers stand on a large pedestal. They look like they are passing through the archway after winning a battle. In front of the Memorial is the Tomb of the Unknown Soldier.

Complete each sentence with the **correct** word or words from the story.

1. The National War Memorial is found in the city of _____.

2. It was built for all the _____ men and women who died in the war.

3. The monument is made out of _____ and has an _____.

4. Two large _____ stand on top of the archway.

5. _____ soldiers stand on a pedestal in the archway.

6. In front of the National War Memorial is the _____ of the _____ Soldier

7. The figures on the top of the archway stand for _____ and _____.

Remembrance Day Reading

Tomb of the Unknown Soldier

On May 23, 2000 a Canadian Forces aircraft flew to France to bring back the remains of the Unknown Soldier to Canada. This Unknown Soldier died in battle overseas more than 80 years ago at Vimy Ridge in France.

The casket carrying the remains of the Unknown Soldier was placed in the Hall of Honour in the Parliament Buildings. He laid in state for three days so that Canadians could see the casket and pay their respects.

On May 28th, the Unknown Soldier was placed on a horse-drawn gun carriage and taken to the National War Memorial. Hundreds of Veterans from the First and Second World Wars, the Prime Minister and the Governor General walked behind the coffin. Thousands of people lined the streets in Ottawa to honour the nameless soldier. The coffin was placed in a granite sarcophagus. The veterans poured in soil from each of Canada's provinces and territories along with soil from the cemetery in France. The Tomb of the Unknown Soldier honours more than 116 000 Canadians who gave their lives for peace and freedom.

Number the sentences in the **correct** order.

_____ Canadians passed by the casket to pay their respects.

_____ At the National War Memorial the coffin was put in a granite sarcophagus.

_____ A plane flew to France to bring back the Unknown Soldier.

_____ Soil from every province and territory in Canada was poured in by veterans.

_____ Veterans, soldiers and important people followed behind the casket.

_____ The casket of the Unknown Soldier was put on a horse-drawn gun carriage and taken to the National War Memorial.

_____ The casket of the Unknown Soldier was put in the Hall of Honour for three days.

Remembrance Day Reading

The Peace Tower

The Peace Tower is found on Parliament Hill in Ottawa is a free-standing bell tower located in front of the Centre Block of the Parliament Buildings. It was built to honour Canadian soldiers who died in World War I. The Tower stands 90.6 metres high. It has a clock with four faces and a group of 53 bells of different sizes. The bells are often heard on special days.

Inside the Tower is a room called the Memorial Chamber. On an altar in the Chamber are the Books of Remembrance. The name of each Canadian soldier who died during a war is found in a Book of Remembrance. Each page of each book is turned once a year, on the same date each year.

Circle the correct answer to each question.

1. In which Canadian city is the Peace Tower found?
    a) Montreal   **b)** Edmonton   **c)** Ottawa   **d)** Vancouver

2. How tall is the Peace Tower?
    a) 100 metres   **b)** 89.6 metres   **c)** 59 metres   **d)** 90.6 metres

3. How many faces does its clock have?
    a) ten   **b)** seven   **c)** four   **d)** six

4. How many bells are in the Tower?
    a) 73   **b)** 53   **c)** 63   **d)** 43

5. What is the name of the special room in the Tower?
    a) Hall of Honour   **b)** War Memories
    c) Remembrance Room   **d)** Memorial Chamber

6. What is written in the Book of Remembrance?
    a) names of airplanes   **b)** names of soldiers
    c) names of battles   **d)** names of ships

Remembrance Day Reading

The Remembrance Day Service

World War I came to an end at eleven o'clock on November 11 in 1918. This day was chosen to remember those who died in the war. It was called "Armistice Day". In 1933, the government changed the name to Remembrance Day.

In Ottawa, a special service is held at the National War Memorial and the Tomb of the Unknown Soldier. Veterans and soldiers parade around the cenotaph. Bands play and choirs sing hymns. When the clock in the Peace Tower strikes eleven o'clock, the bugler plays the "Last Post" and the flag bearers lower their flags.

The Two-Minute Silence begins when a gun is fired. People bow their heads in prayer. The silence is ended when the bugler plays "Reveille". The flags are raised, the bands play, and wreaths are placed on the Tomb of the Unknown Soldier. The service ends with everyone singing "O Canada".

When did it happen?

Print the word **before** or the word **after** in each sentence.

1. The Peace Tower clock strikes eleven o'clock _____ the bugler plays the Last Post.

2. The veterans and soldiers parade around the cenotaph _____ the service begins.

3. Everyone sings O Canada _____ the wreaths are placed on the Tomb of the Unknown Soldier.

4. The band plays and the choirs sing _____ the Peace Tower clocks strikes eleven o'clock.

5. The Two-Minute Silence begins _____ the gun is fired.

6. The bugler plays Reveille _____ the Two-Minute Silence.

Remembrance Day Reading

Billy Barker

Billy Barker was one of the greatest fighter pilots of World War I. He was born in Dauphin, Manitoba. As a boy he enjoyed horseback riding, shooting and hunting birds. He joined the army in 1915 and became a machine gunner. After spending time in the awful trenches in France, he decided to go into the Royal Canadian Airforce. Billy flew a plane called the Sopwith Camel which he made famous. He flew on many raids and missions with his squadron. Billy liked to fly low to the ground making the enemy planes fly low and then he would shoot upwards into the fuselage.

Billy Barker and his squadron destroyed many enemy airbases and shot down many enemy airplanes. In the last month of the war, he performed his most famous feat. On his way back to England, all by himself, he took on 60 enemy planes. During these battles he was shot three times and passed out twice. Barker was able to shoot down five of the planes before he crash-landed, skidding sideways and then flipping over. He was rescued by some Scottish soldiers who had watched the spectacular air battle. Billy survived the crash and was awarded the Victoria Cross for his bravery during this air battle.

Is it true or False?

Print **True** or **False** on the line at the end of each sentence.

1. Billy Barker was a famous Canadian sailor. _____

2. Billy joined the army first and then became a pilot. _____

3. Billy Barker flew a plane called the Sopwith Camel. _____

4. Billy Barker would dive and shoot at enemy planes. _____

5. Barker met sixty planes on his way back to England. _____

6. He shot down ten of the planes on his way back to England. _____

7. Even though Billy was shot three times and passed out twice, he kept on fighting. _____

8. Billy Barker was killed when his plane crashed in a field. _____

Remembrance Day Reading

Billy Bishop

Billy Bishop was one of Canada's most famous air aces of World War I. He was born in Owen Sound Ontario. When he was seventeen, his parents sent him to the Royal Military College in Kingston, Ontario. They hoped he would become a better student. His schooling was cut short as World War I was beginning.

Billy Bishop joined the army and was sent to England. Fighting in the trenches made him unhappy so he decided to join the Royal Canadian Airforce to become a pilot. Billy often went flying all alone in enemy countries. He would make surprise attacks on German air bases. Billy became famous for shooting down 72 enemy planes during the war. He was given the Victoria Cross as well as other medals for his bravery.

Complete each sentence with the **correct** word or words from the story.

1. Billy Bishop was a _____ who flew planes during World War _____.

2. He joined the airforce because he did not like to fight in the _____.

3. During World War I, Billy became a _____ air _____.

4. He liked to fly _____ and make _____ attacks on enemy air bases.

5. During the war he shot down _____ planes.

6. The _____ Cross medal was given to him for his _____.

Remembrance Day Reading

A. Roy Brown

A. Roy Brown was born in Carleton Place, Ontario. He was a fighter pilot during World War I. During the war, he was the pilot who shot down Germany's famous fighter pilot nicknamed the "Red Baron". His real name was Manfred von Richthofen.

On April 21, 1918, British and German pilots took off in their planes on fighting missions. A. Roy Brown saw the German planes first. He told a new pilot named Wop May to stay up high in the sky and out of danger while he led his squadron to the attack. Before long, Brown had two German planes on his tail. Wop May saw what was happening and couldn't wait so he dove down to attack the planes. He shot bullets all over the sky but missed everything and both of his guns jammed. Wop May decided to head for the air base. The Red Baron spotted Wop May leaving and followed him. A. Roy Brown saw what was happening and followed the Red Baron firing at his plane. At the same time Australian gunners were firing from the ground. Their bullets also hit the Red Baron's plane. The plane wobbled and nosed into the ground killing the Red Baron.

Number the folowing sentences in the **correct** order.

_____ Two German planes followed A. Roy Brown.

_____ British and German planes were flying in the sky.

_____ Wop May couldn't wait so he dove and shot at the planes.

_____ A. Roy Brown spotted the German planes.

_____ When his guns jammed, Wop may headed to the base and the Red Baron followed him.

_____ A. Roy Brown flew after the Red Baron firing at his plane.

_____ The plane crashed killing the Red Baron.

_____ A. Roy Brown told Wop may to stay up high and out of danger.

_____ Bullets from guns on the ground hit the Red Baron's plane as well.

Remembrance Day Reading

John McCrae

John Mc Crae was born in Guelph, Ontario, in 1872. He went to university to become a doctor. John also liked to write poetry and some of his poems were published in magazines and newspapers.

During World War I, he joined the army. He became a major and a surgeon. John was stationed in Flanders during the spring of 1915. One of his close friends was killed in a battle near Flanders. The next day another soldier saw him sitting on the step of an ambulance writing on a pad of paper. John kept looking at his friend's grave. The poem that he wrote was about what he saw that day. There were larks flying in the sky while guns were booming. Poppies were fluttering in the breeze between the crosses on the graves of the dead soldiers. The poem that he wrote that day was called "In Flanders Fields". This poem has made John McCrae famous all over the world.

Circle the answer or answers to each question.

1. In which city was John McCrae born?
   a) Hamilton   **b)** Toronto   **c)** Kingston   **d)** Guelph

2. What did he become?
   a) dentist   **b)** doctor   **c)** teacher   **d)** lawyer

3. What did John McCrae enjoy writing?
   a) stories   **b)** riddles   **c)** poems   **d)** plays

4. Where was John stationed during the war?
   a) Paris   **b)** London   **c)** Rome   **d)** Flanders

5. How do you think John McCrae felt when he looked at his friend's grave?
   a) happy   **b)** surprised   **c)** excited   **d)** sad

6. What were the things he saw and heard that day?
   sunflowers   poppies   guns   tanks   crosses   graves
   robins   airplanes   larks   bombs   boats   soldiers

Remembrance Day Riddles

Read each riddle carefully. **Print** the answer on the line provided.

1. I am a war vehicle.
    I travel on land.
    I am made of metal.
    Soldiers can travel inside me.
    I am a _____.

2. It grew in Flanders Fields.
    It is a bright red flower.
    We wear one on
    Remembrance Day.
    It is a _____.

3. It is a war vehicle.
    It travels in the air.
    It has wings and a tail.
    It is an _____.

4. We fought in wars too.
    We sailed in warships and
    submarines.
    We were always looking for
    enemy ships.
    We were _____.

5. It is a war vehicle.
    It can travel on the water and
    under the water.
    It shoots torpedoes to destroy
    enemy ships.
    It is a _____.

6. I am round in shape.
    I am made of poppies and
    oak leaves.
    I am put on a cenotaph.
    I am a _____.

7. This war vehicle travels on the
    ocean.
    It carries soldiers to battlefields.
    Sailors shoot guns to destroy
    enemy ships.
    It is a _____.

8. These men fought on land.
    They had to fight from trenches.
    Many of them died during a
    war.
    They are _____.

Remembrance Day Riddles

Read each riddle carefully. **Print** the answer on the line provided.

1. We flew in small planes
   We dropped bombs on cities.
   We shot down many enemy
   planes.
   Some of us were war heroes.
   We were _____.

2. I was once a soldier.
   I fought in World War Two.
   Now I sell poppies for
   Remembrance Day.
   I walk in parades too.
   I am a war _____.

3. I was built out of stone.
   I stand in a special place for
   all to see.
   Names of those who died in
   the wars are written on me.
   I am a _____.

4. I am a special building in
   Ottawa.
   I was built to honour Canadian
   troops.
   I have a clock and 53 bells.
   I am the _____.

5. It is a special cemetery.
   Many soldiers are buried there.
   Poppies grew on their graves.
   There are rows of white
   crosses.
   It is _____.

6. I play a special horn on
   Remembrance Day.
   I play the Last Post.
   Everyone bows their heads in
   silence.
   I am a _____.

7. I am a gentle bird.
   I am pure white in colour.
   I am often used as a symbol
   of peace.
   I am a _____.

8. It is a special grave.
   The grave holds the Unknown
   Soldier.
   It can be found in front of the
   National War memorial.
   It is the _____
   _____

Skill: Writing a Letter

Write a **letter** to a present-day military person thanking him or her for the things they do to keep Canada and the world a safe place to live.

Dear ______________________________

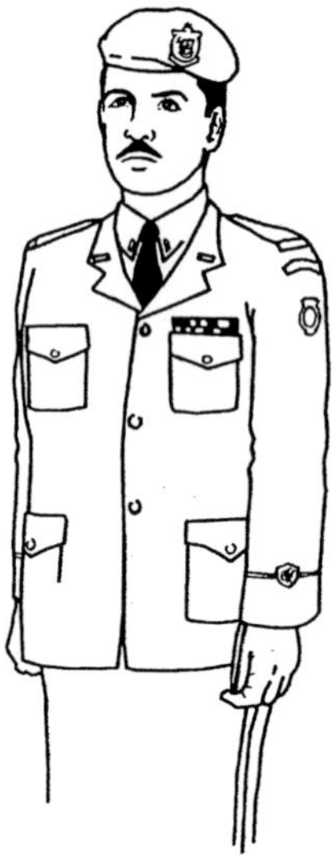

Yours Truly

____

Remembrance Day

Lest We Forget

Name: _____

National War Memorial

_____

_____

_____

_____

_____

Tomb of the Unknown Soldier

Remembrance Day Service

_____

_____

_____

_____

_____

The Poppy

_____

_____

_____

_____

_____

_____

_____

_____

_____

The Peace Tower

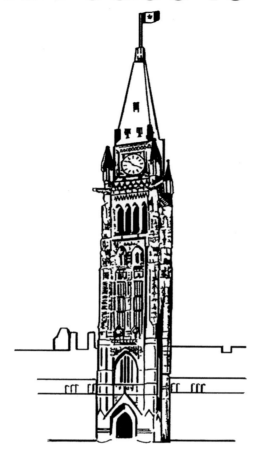

A Veteran

A Bugler

_____

_____

_____

_____

_____

_____

Soldiers, Sailors, Airmen

_____

_____

_____

_____

_____

_____

_____

_____

Answer Key

Initial Consonant Pp: *(page 25)*
The pictures coloured red should be: pail, pool, pencil, pumpkin, porcupine, pig, peanut, pot

Review of Initial Consonants: *(page 26)*
Row 1: p, b, t   **Row 2:** m, p, s   **Row 3:** m, s, p   **Row 4:** b, d, b

Blend Cr: *(page 27)*
Pictures to be circled: crab, crate, crocodile, crane, cradle, crown, crayon,

Long Vowel Sounds: *(page 28)*
Words to be coloured green: peace, bugle, sailor, brave, pilot, hero, silence, soldiers, grave, field, pray, praise

Short Vowel Sounds: *(page 29)*
Poppies to be coloured red: bands, dead, cross, tank, guns, ships

Blend Fl: *(page 30)*
Row 1: f, fl, f   **Row 2:** fl, f, f   **Row 3:** f, fl f

Initial Consonant Mm: *(page 31)*
Pictures to be coloured yellow: mask, mice, money, matches, mushroom, mirror, moon

Sounds S, Sh, Sl: *(page 32)*
Row 1: s, sl, sh, s   **Row 2:** sh, s, sh, sl   **Row 3:** sh, s, sh, s

Blend Pl: *(page 33)*
Row 1: p, pl, p, pr   **Row 2:** pl, p, p, pl   **Row 3:** p, pr, pl, p

Initial Consonant Dd: *(page 34)*
Row 1: b, c, d, p   **Row 2:** c, d, b, d   **Row 3:** p, d, c, b

Syllabication: *(page 39)*
One Syllable Words: war, cross, peace, dove, wreath
Two Syllable Words: bugler, poppy, army, hero, parades
Three Syllable Words: November, remember, veterans, uniforms, memory

Word Search: *(page 40)*

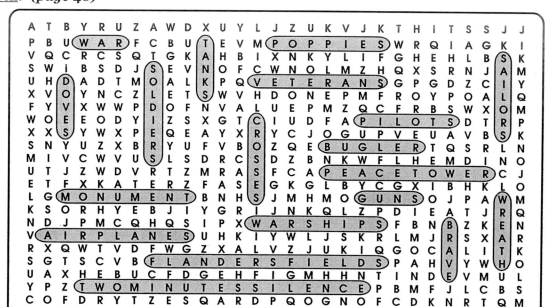

Antonyms: *(page 41)*

1. remember, forget
2. die, live
3. peace, war
4. brave, afraid
5. build, destroy
6. noisy, silent
7. Young, old
8. friends, enemies
9. won, lost
10. men, women

Synonyms: *(page 42)*

1. songs
2. mean
3. quietly
4. graveyard
5. hurt
6. cenotaphs
7. troops
8. airmen
9. friends
10. costumes

Homonyms: *(page 43)*

1. war
2. wear
3. Peace
4. son
5. died
6. sea
7. led
8. plane
9. week
10. pause

Rhyming Words: *(page 44)*

1. cross, boss, toss
2. fight, light, right
3. brave, grave, save
4. dove, glove, love
5. tank, bank, sank, thank
6. sailor, tailor, trailer
7. shoot, hoot, boot
8. navy, wavy, gravy
9. band, sand, hand, land
10. bells, shells, smells, swells

Crossword Puzzle: *(page 45)*

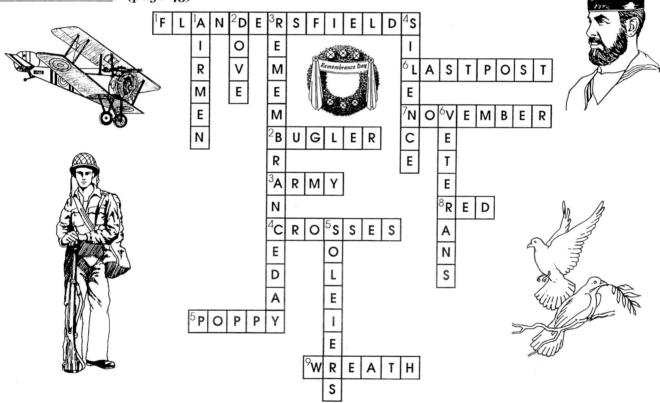

Singular and Plural Words: *(page 47)*

1. Poppies
2. Armies
3. woman
4. soldier
5. trenches
6. Veterans
7. crosses
8. Cemeteries
9. torpedoes
10. heroes

Writing Sentences: *(page 48)*

1. Billy Bishop shot down 72 enemy planes.
2. John McCrae wrote the poem In Flanders Fields.
3. War veterans sell poppies for Remembrance Day.
4. Remembrance Day is held on November eleventh.
5. Poppies are bright, red flowers that grow in Flanders Fields.
6. The bugler plays the Last Post at eleven o'clock.

Remembrance Day Thoughts: *(page 49)*
Answers will vary

Identifying Causes: *(page 55)*
The following causes should have check marks.

pushing in line; telling on someone; not sharing; playing a mean trick on someone; calling someone names; hitting someone; tripping someone; making someone cry; making fun of someone's clothes; making fun of someone's looks; breaking someone's toy; saying mean things about someone; telling lies; yelling angrily a your friends; pulling someone's hair

Classifying Sentences: *(page 56)*
The following sentences should have check marks: 2, 4, 6, 7, 8, 10, 12, 13, 14

Recalling Details: *(page 57)*
   1. No   **2.** Yes   **3.** Yes   **4.** No   **5.** No   **6.** Yes

Context Clues: *(page 58)*
   1. Ottawa   **2.** Canadian   **3.** stone, archway   **4.** figures   **5.** 25   **6.** Tomb, Unknown

Sequencing Events: *(page 59)*
3, 6, 1, 7, 5, 4, 2

Noting Detail: *(page 60)*
   1. c   **2.** c   **3.** c   **4.** b   **5.** d   **6.** b

Sequencing Events: *(page 61)*
   1. before   **2.** before   **3.** after   **4.** before   **5.** after   **6.** after

Drawing Conclusions: *(page 62)*
   1. False   **2.** True   **3.** True   **4.** False   **5.** True   **6.** False
   7. True   **8.** False

Context Clues: *(page 63)*
   1. pilot, One   **2.** trenches   **3.** famous, ace   **4.** alone, surprise   **5.** 72
   6. Victoria, bravery

Sequencing Events: *(page 64)*
4, 1, 5, 2, 6, 7, 9, 3, 8

Recalling Details: *(page 65)*
   1. d   **2.** b   **3.** c   **4.** d   **5.** d   **6.** poppies, guns, crosses, graves, larks, soldiers

Finding the Main Idea: *(page 66)*
   1. tank   **2.** poppy   **3.** airplane   **4.** sailors   **5.** submarine
   6. wreath   **7.** warship   **8.** soldiers

Finding the Main Idea: *(page 67)*
   1. pilots   **2.** veterans   **3.** cenotaph   **4.** Peace Tower   **5.** Flanders Fields
   6. bugler   **7.** dove   **8.** Tomb of the Unknown Soldier

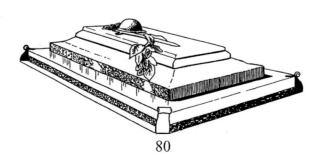